How to win your wife's heart

by

Ibraahim Ibn Saaleh al-Mahmud

Al-Firdous Ltd, London

2000: First Edition
2012: Revised Edition

Typeset by Abu Yusuf.

ISBN 1 874263 21 3

Published and Distributed by:
Al-Firdous Ltd.
10, Fonthill Road, London
N4 3HX

Email:al_firdous@hotmail.co.uk
www.al-firdous.co.uk

Printed by: Mega Print
Baha Is Merkezi

HaramideEre, Istanbul

Table of Contents

بسم الله الرحمن الرحيم

How to win your wife's heart

by: Ibraahim Ibn Saaleh al-Mahmud

Introduction

All praise is due to Allah who says:

وَمِنْ ءَايَٰتِهِۦٓ أَنْ خَلَقَ لَكُم مِّنْ أَنفُسِكُمْ أَزْوَٰجًا
لِّتَسْكُنُوٓا۟ إِلَيْهَا وَجَعَلَ بَيْنَكُم مَّوَدَّةً وَرَحْمَةً ۚ إِنَّ فِى
ذَٰلِكَ لَءَايَٰتٍ لِّقَوْمٍ يَتَفَكَّرُونَ ﴿٢١﴾

"And among His signs is this, that He created for you wives from among yourselves, that you may find repose in them, and He has put between you affection and mercy" [Surah *Ar-Rum*:verse 21],

and Peace and Blessing be upon our prophet Muhammad who said: "The best of you is one who is best with one's household (in treatment) and I am best of you to my household", reported by *At-Tirmidih* and others.

To proceed:

Today, if we look at people's lives we will be disappointed

and feel distressed because sins, forbidden actions and misdeeds have become widespread. Concepts that were once common among some people have changed, the evil has become the good and the good has become the evil. Traditions and ethics have also changed.

Accordingly, people become influenced and fascinated by the ideas of Western "civilization" and affected by dirty and indecent movies which look at betrayal as love, disintegration as freedom and openness, respect for the husband as backwardness and complexity and the understanding between the husband and wife as weakness. As a result, misfortunes have increased, disasters diffused and Muslims have become tense and confused.

- The wife does not fulfill the rights of her husband!
- The husband ignores and oppresses his wife!
- The children are disobedient to their parents!
- The parents ignore their children's education!

These problems are only caused by Muslims' disobedience to Allah's rules.

In order to help in the construction of the ideal Muslim home, I have prepared this paper

“How to win your wife's heart”

It is among the series of the happy Muslim family, its aim is to create a solid, sincere and understanding **Muslim family**, reigned by admiration, respect, love, commitment, mental tranquility and happiness.

Whose slogan is: religion is sincerity.

Whose Goal is: a right education for the children.

Whose Reference is: the Qur'an, the Sunnah and the sayings of the worthy ancestors.

Whose Aspiration is: that they will be called on the Day of Judgment to:

ٱدْخُلُوا۟ ٱلْجَنَّةَ أَنتُمْ وَأَزْوَٰجُكُمْ تُحْبَرُونَ ﴿٧٠﴾ يُطَافُ عَلَيْهِم بِصِحَافٍ مِّن ذَهَبٍ وَأَكْوَابٍ ۖ وَفِيهَا مَا تَشْتَهِيهِ ٱلْأَنفُسُ وَتَلَذُّ ٱلْأَعْيُنُ ۖ وَأَنتُمْ فِيهَا خَٰلِدُونَ ﴿٧١﴾

Enter Paradise, you and your wives, in happiness. Trays of gold and cups will be passed round them,

(there will be) therein all that the one's inner selves could desire, all that the eyes could delight in, and you will abide therein forever. [*Az-zukhruf*: 70 -71].

Whose Model is: the Prophet (ﷺ), his companions, the followers and those who follow his footsteps with sincerity till the Day of Judgement.

Among other reasons that prompted me to prepare this paper is the increase in the number of divorce cases and of marriage problems, the negligence of each partner's rights towards the other and the low esteem that some husbands show towards their wives. For example, some men, may Allah guide them, do not fulfill their wives' rights and do not care about them. They raise their voices for no reason, do not share with their wives the good and bad things and prefer to spend the night with their friends and travel than to look after their families and their wives. Accordingly, their behaviour leads the wives to live in a state of anxiety, distress and misery and destroy their spirits. So, to those men I am addressing this paper.

I say:

A woman is weak, affectionate, emotional and cannot bear a man when raising his voice and showing his muscles. She needs his care all the time. She needs affection, compassion, a smile and true love. She needs safe direction and the right advice, and she needs to be addressed with wisdom, tenderness and the proper style because she is the mother of the children. She is the school that was once spoken of thus:

The mother is a school if you look after her,

you will get a people of noble descent

The mother is like a garden if showered

with water, it will put forth abundant leaves

The mother is the master of all teachers

She occupies their glorious deeds in all horizons

This letter is also addressed:

- To anyone who wants to live a peaceful, happy, meaningful and a pleasant life.
- To anyone who wants to lead his married life in the right path and to Paradise.
- To anyone who wants to make his house a model for marital happiness and a school to raise pious and righteous offspring.
- To anyone who wants to make his house a cultural source for calling people to follow the commandments of Allah and for enjoining good and forbidding evil.

So, it is appropriate for us to improve our characters and our behavior towards our wives, and offer them what Allah ﷻ has obliged us with trust and loyalty. I ask Allah to grant us all happiness in this world and in the Hereafter, and may the Blessing and Peace of Allah be upon our beloved prophet Muhammad (ﷺ).

30 Ways
To Achieve
HAPPINESS
Aidh Ibn Abdullah Al-Qarni

Treating Woman with Kindness

Allah ﷻ says:

يَٰٓأَيُّهَا ٱلَّذِينَ ءَامَنُواْ لَا يَحِلُّ لَكُمْ أَن تَرِثُواْ ٱلنِّسَآءَ كَرْهًاۖ وَلَا تَعْضُلُوهُنَّ لِتَذْهَبُواْ بِبَعْضِ مَآ ءَاتَيْتُمُوهُنَّ إِلَّآ أَن يَأْتِينَ بِفَٰحِشَةٍ مُّبَيِّنَةٍۚ وَعَاشِرُوهُنَّ بِٱلْمَعْرُوفِۚ فَإِن كَرِهْتُمُوهُنَّ فَعَسَىٰٓ أَن تَكْرَهُواْ شَيْـًٔا وَيَجْعَلَ ٱللَّهُ فِيهِ خَيْرًا كَثِيرًا ﴿١٩﴾

And live with them honorably, [*An-Nisaa*:19].

The prophet ﷺ said: "Act kindly towards women for the woman has been created from a rib and the most crooked part of a rib is its upper part. So, if you attempt to straighten it, you will break it but if you leave it, its crookedness will remain there. So act kindly towards women" [agreed upon].

The prophet ﷺ also said: "Beware, act kindly towards women. For they are married women with you. You have no right over them except this that they commit some obvious abomination. Then, if they commit that, leave them in beds (alone) and give them a beating without molesting (them). If, they obey you, do not then seek some excuse against them".[1]

"Many of us have heard stories of men treating their wives badly as if they were slaves of an oppressive master, they insulted and tormented them, and in some incidents they even beat their faces, as a result the house becomes an unbearable hell".[2] This behavior is not a quality of the pious men. Islam has forbidden such conduct, and the last command of the Prophet ﷺ was:

" ...Act kindly towards women", [agreed upon].

Mua'wiya Ibn Ubayda (may Allah be pleased with him) reported, I said; "Allah's messenger, what is the right of the wife if one of us comes upon her?", the Prophet ﷺ replied, "It is that you feed her when you take food and provide her clothes when you clothe yourself and that you do not beat her face, nor revile her ; nor leave her alone except in the house"[3]

Muslim Brother, I remind you to be gentle to your wife, treat her nicely and respect her, particularly in front of the children, because if you underestimate her personality, you might cause serious consequences. The Prophet ﷺ said: "The most perfect of the believers in faith is he who is the most excellent of them in morals and the best of you are they who

---

[1] Reported by *At-Tirmidih.*

[2] "Nahwa Usratin Muslimatin" by *Istanbuli.*

[3] Reported by Ahmed, Abu Daawud and Ibnu Ma'ja.

are best for their wives"[4]

Brother, do not look for perfection in this universe; but accept what is best! And haven't you thought about yourself whether you are perfect or not. In reality, we are all in the same position, there is no need to demand perfection from others while we are drowned in our own flaws and shortcomings, seizing the opportunity of the woman's weakness and need. If we were stronger than her, Allah is stronger than us. The Prophet ﷺ said: "A believer must not hate a believing woman. If he dislikes any of her characteristics, he will be pleased with another one"[5].

A man asked al-Hassan Ibnu Ali, may Allah be pleased with them, "I have a daughter and she is getting married, to whom shall I give her? Al-Hassan Ibnu Ali then replied: "Marry her to someone who fears Allah, if he loves her, he will be kind to her. If he dislikes her, he will not treat her unjustly"[6]

---

[4] Reported by *at-Tirmidih* who categorized it as *Hasan.*

[5] Reported by *Muslim*

[6] *al-iqdul Fareed*

The Islamic Concept
Of
Justice
Written by: Umar Ahmed Kassir

The Wife's Rights.

The wife has several rights over her husband. Allah سبحانه وتعالى says:

وَٱلْمُطَلَّقَٰتُ يَتَرَبَّصْنَ بِأَنفُسِهِنَّ ثَلَٰثَةَ قُرُوٓءٍ ۚ وَلَا
يَحِلُّ لَهُنَّ أَن يَكْتُمْنَ مَا خَلَقَ ٱللَّهُ فِىٓ أَرْحَامِهِنَّ إِن كُنَّ
يُؤْمِنَّ بِٱللَّهِ وَٱلْيَوْمِ ٱلْءَاخِرِ ۚ وَبُعُولَتُهُنَّ أَحَقُّ بِرَدِّهِنَّ فِى
ذَٰلِكَ إِنْ أَرَادُوٓا۟ إِصْلَٰحًا ۚ وَلَهُنَّ مِثْلُ ٱلَّذِى عَلَيْهِنَّ
بِٱلْمَعْرُوفِ ۚ وَلِلرِّجَالِ عَلَيْهِنَّ دَرَجَةٌ ۗ وَٱللَّهُ عَزِيزٌ حَكِيمٌ

﴿٢٢٨﴾

"And they (women) have rights over their husbands similar to those of their husbands over them to what is reasonable, but men have a degree of responsibility over them". [*Al-Baqarah*:228].

The Prophet ﷺ said: "You, men have rights over your wives

and they have rights over you"[7]. A companion of the Prophet ﷺ reported, I said: "Allah's messenger, what is the right of the wife if anyone of us comes upon her?", He replied, "It is that you feed her when you take food and provide her clothes when you clothe yourself and that you do not beat her face, nor revile her; nor leave her alone except in the house"[8] The Prophet ﷺ said: "In the Day of Judgement the fair minded will be upon a dais of light on the right of the Most Beneficent, those who act justly in their judgement, among their family and people"[9]. Ibnu ab-Baas said: "I like to adorn myself for my wife as I want her to adorn herself for me".

Other rights of the wife:

1- good company, Allah ﷻ says:

يَٰٓأَيُّهَا ٱلَّذِينَ ءَامَنُواْ لَا يَحِلُّ لَكُمۡ أَن تَرِثُواْ ٱلنِّسَآءَ كَرۡهٗاۖ
وَلَا تَعۡضُلُوهُنَّ لِتَذۡهَبُواْ بِبَعۡضِ مَآ ءَاتَيۡتُمُوهُنَّ إِلَّآ أَن
يَأۡتِينَ بِفَٰحِشَةٖ مُّبَيِّنَةٖۚ وَعَاشِرُوهُنَّ بِٱلۡمَعۡرُوفِۚ فَإِن
كَرِهۡتُمُوهُنَّ فَعَسَىٰٓ أَن تَكۡرَهُواْ شَيۡـٔٗا وَيَجۡعَلَ ٱللَّهُ فِيهِ
خَيۡرٗا كَثِيرٗا ١٩

[7] Reported by *at-Tirmidih* and categorized it as *Sahih.*

[8] Reported by *Abu Daawud* and others

[9] Reported by *Muslim*

"And live with them honourably", [*an-Nisa*:19].

2- education, we should teach a woman everything she needs regarding *deen* .

3- enjoining the good on her and forbidding the evil. Allah ﷻ says:

وَأْمُرْ أَهْلَكَ بِٱلصَّلَوٰةِ وَٱصْطَبِرْ عَلَيْهَا ۖ لَا نَسْـَٔلُكَ رِزْقًا ۖ نَّحْنُ نَرْزُقُكَ ۗ وَٱلْعَـٰقِبَةُ لِلتَّقْوَىٰ ﴿١٣٢﴾

"And enjoin prayer on your family, and be patient in offering them (the prayers)" [*Taha*:132]

and:

يَـٰٓأَيُّهَا ٱلَّذِينَ ءَامَنُوا۟ قُوٓا۟ أَنفُسَكُمْ وَأَهْلِيكُمْ نَارًا وَقُودُهَا ٱلنَّاسُ وَٱلْحِجَارَةُ عَلَيْهَا مَلَـٰٓئِكَةٌ غِلَاظٌ شِدَادٌ لَّا يَعْصُونَ ٱللَّهَ مَآ أَمَرَهُمْ وَيَفْعَلُونَ مَا يُؤْمَرُونَ ﴿٦﴾

"O you who believe! Ward off from yourselves and your families a fire (hell) whose fuel is men and stones"

[*at-Tahrim*:6]

4- moderation in jealousy.

5- dowry, Allah ﷻ says:

وَءَاتُوا۟ ٱلنِّسَآءَ صَدُقَـٰتِهِنَّ نِحْلَةً ۚ فَإِن طِبْنَ لَكُمْ عَن شَىْءٍ
مِّنْهُ نَفْسًا فَكُلُوهُ هَنِيٓـًٔا مَّرِيٓـًٔا ﴿٤﴾

"And give to the women (whom you marry) their dowry with a good heart, but if they, of their own good pleasure, remit any part of it to you, take it, and enjoy it without fear of any harm (as Allah has made it lawful)" [*an-Nisa*:4].

6- support, Allah ﷻ says:

۞ وَٱلْوَٰلِدَٰتُ يُرْضِعْنَ أَوْلَـٰدَهُنَّ حَوْلَيْنِ كَامِلَيْنِ ۖ لِمَنْ
أَرَادَ أَن يُتِمَّ ٱلرَّضَاعَةَ ۚ وَعَلَى ٱلْمَوْلُودِ لَهُۥ رِزْقُهُنَّ
وَكِسْوَتُهُنَّ بِٱلْمَعْرُوفِ ۚ لَا تُكَلَّفُ نَفْسٌ إِلَّا وُسْعَهَا ۚ لَا
تُضَآرَّ وَٰلِدَةٌۢ بِوَلَدِهَا وَلَا مَوْلُودٌ لَّهُۥ بِوَلَدِهِۦ ۚ وَعَلَى
ٱلْوَارِثِ مِثْلُ ذَٰلِكَ ۗ فَإِنْ أَرَادَا فِصَالًا عَن تَرَاضٍ مِّنْهُمَا
وَتَشَاوُرٍ فَلَا جُنَاحَ عَلَيْهِمَا ۗ وَإِنْ أَرَدتُّمْ أَن تَسْتَرْضِعُوٓا۟

أَوْلَـٰدَكُمْ فَلَا جُنَاحَ عَلَيْكُمْ إِذَا سَلَّمْتُم مَّآ ءَاتَيْتُم بِٱلْمَعْرُوفِ ۗ وَٱتَّقُوا۟ ٱللَّهَ وَٱعْلَمُوٓا۟ أَنَّ ٱللَّهَ بِمَا تَعْمَلُونَ بَصِيرٌ ﴿٢٣٣﴾

"but the father of the child shall bear the cost of the mother's food and clothing on a reasonable basis. No person shall have a burden laid on him greater than he can bear" [*Al-Baqara*:233].

The Prophet ﷺ said: "It is a sufficient sin for a woman that she wastes the sustenance", agreed upon.

7- fairness in division if one has more than one wife, the Prophet ﷺ said: "If a man has two wives and does not deal equitably between them, he will come on the Day of Resurrection while his one side will be hanging down"[10]

8- to stop treating her badly and to respect her feelings. The Prophet ﷺ used to help his family; he used to mend his shoes, patch his clothes and sweep the floor[11]

9- not to divulge her secrets, nor mention her flaws, the Prophet ﷺ said: "The worst of mankind in rank in the sight of Allah on the Day of Resurrection is the man who has sexual intercourse (Jimaa) with his wife and then he divulges her

---

[10] Reported by *Ahmed* and others.

[11] Al-Hadeeth, agreed upon.

secrets."[12].

10- to allow her to visit her parents, her family and her neighbours.

11- to protect his wife against mixing with women engaged in evil talk and deeds or those of ill repute, and not to allow her to buy indecent magazines and dirty movies.

12- not to spend the night out till late, the Prophet ﷺ said: "your wife has rights over you"[13]

13- not to seek to take his wife's wages if she is working, nor her wealth if she inherits, because this will annoy her and spoil her life and eventually she will give up her wages or part of it, or some of her wealth unwillingly.

---

[12] Reported by *Muslim*

[13] Reported by *Al-Bukhaari*.

Rights common to husband and wife

1- to overlook mistakes and errors, particularly, the unintentional ones.

2- emotional participation in happiness and sorrow.

3- to give each other sincere advice.

4- not to divulge each others secrets, nor speak ill of each other before people.

5- to live honourably, this will protect their chastity.

6- to dress nicely.

7- to appreciate and respect each other.

8- to educate their children according to Islamic teachings. The parents should be concerned about their children's education, particularly their daughters. The Prophet ﷺ said: "He who brings up two girls properly until they have grown up, he and I would come (very close) on the Day of Resurrection, and he interlaced his fingers (for explaining the point of nearness between him and that one.)"[14] Therefore, we should take into consideration the following points:

---

[14] Reported by *Muslim*

- encouraging the girls to wear Hijab.
- discouraging them from dressing indecently.
- occupying their spare time with useful Islamic books and cassettes.
- avoid buying tapes of music and music instruments.
- avoid buying dirty and indecent magazines of artists, footballers and clubs.

Treating the wife with kindness

The wife has to be loved by her husband. He should call her by her best name and treat her with deference. He has to treat her family kindly by praising them in front of her, exchange visits and invite them in every occasion. Also, he has to listen to her, respect her opinion, and accept her advice if it was right. In short, any matter considered in our *Deen* and tradition to be good should be adopted in their marriage relation.

In addition, he has to show noble character, endure her problems and show clemency in time of her recklessness and anger; more than that he has to joke and play with her because this makes her cheerful. The Prophet ﷺ used to joke with his wives. Omar ﷺ said: "A man should be like a child with his wives, but if they need him, he should act like a man".

The husband should have a sense of humour to cheer his wife, soothe her pains and to relieve her of the burdens of life and work because all this will strengthen the bonds of love and respect between them.

The Veil
Evidence of Niqab

Dr. Muhammed Ibn Ahmed Ibn Ismail

The Causes of Marriage Problems

1- sins and misdeeds

2- negligence

3- irresponsibility

4- relatives interference

5- reprehensible jealousy

6- devilish insinuation

7- interference in other's business

8- the exertion of authority of one of the couple.

9- distrust

10- misunderstanding of each other's character and mental non-congruence

11- false beliefs

12- monotony of everyday life

13- dirty magazines and movies

14- lack of sincerity and truthfulness

15- the influence of neighbours

16- dissatisfaction with worldly matters

17- social class difference

18- education difference

19- age difference

20- mixed gatherings of men and women

21- the preference of some children to others

22- unequal treatment between the wives

23- frequent absence from the house

24- frequent nights out

25- travelling abroad for bad purpose.

The Epidemic of Sins

Sins and forbidden actions are considered to be one of the most serious causes of marriage problems and its spread among Muslims. Allah ﷻ as well as the people attach no importance to a sinner.

Ibnul Qayyim said: "Among the punishments originated from sins is that they revoke the blessings and cause curses. The servant of Allah loses Allah's blessing by a sin, and is inflicted by a curse when he commits a sin".

And among the punishments inflicted on a sinner: He loses his rank, position and dignity towards Allah and His servants, because the most revered person to Allah ﷻ is the one who fears Him most, the closest one to Him is the one who obeys Him in everything, and the position of a servant is established by his submission to Allah's commands. If he disobeys Allah's commands, he will be dropped in His estimation and Allah will also drop him in His servants estimation. Consequently, he will live among them in a bad predicament, underestimated, miserable, unrespected and unhappy.

Some wives often complain about their husbands' sudden change. They reminisce the sweet moments they passed and the love they used to share together; but, now, they do not care anymore about them nor about the children.

Sheikh Ahmad Al-Qattaan said: "The wife is the reason behind her husband's sudden change, she should ask herself and read Allah's saying in the Qu'ran:

لَهُۥ مُعَقِّبَٰتٌ مِّنۢ بَيۡنِ يَدَيۡهِ وَمِنۡ خَلۡفِهِۦ يَحۡفَظُونَهُۥ مِنۡ
أَمۡرِ ٱللَّهِۗ إِنَّ ٱللَّهَ لَا يُغَيِّرُ مَا بِقَوۡمٍ حَتَّىٰ يُغَيِّرُواْ مَا
بِأَنفُسِهِمۡۗ وَإِذَآ أَرَادَ ٱللَّهُ بِقَوۡمٖ سُوٓءٗا فَلَا مَرَدَّ لَهُۥۚ وَمَا
لَهُم مِّن دُونِهِۦ مِن وَالٍ ﴿١١﴾

Verily! Allah will not change the good condition of a people as long as they do not change their state of goodness themselves. [*Ar-Raad*:11].

Perhaps, it is because either she or her husband has committed a sin.

The reasons behind the marriage problems:

- The worst is abandoning prayers and other Islamic obligations such as *Zakat*, fasting and pilgrimage.
- The wife's delay to take a bath so as to keep her hair done.
- Not encouraging their daughters to wear Hijaab when they reach the age of puberty.
- The breaking of relations.
- Hiding the children's wrong doings from their father.
- Backbiting
- Usury
- The watching of dirty movies and listening to music
- Employing a maid and car driver unnecessarily.
- Making fun of religious people and of Islam
- Smoking and drinking intoxicant.
- Disobeying the parents.

Therefore, it is obligatory to examine and correct ourselves, to fulfill our Islamic duties and abstain from forbidden actions, and in Allah's willing, happiness will return to the family and the house.

An Important Fatwa

This question was answered by the scholar Sheikh Abdul Aziz Ibn Baaz after a woman complained about her husband's misbehaviour.

You said in your question that your husband has abandoned prayers and insults the *Deen* . If such is the case, then your husband is a *Kafir* (disbeliever) and it is unlawful to live or stay with him in the same house. So, you have to go to your family or anywhere where you feel safe because Allah ﷻ says:

يَـٰٓأَيُّهَا ٱلَّذِينَ ءَامَنُوٓا۟ إِذَا جَآءَكُمُ ٱلْمُؤْمِنَـٰتُ مُهَـٰجِرَٰتٍ
فَٱمْتَحِنُوهُنَّ ۖ ٱللَّهُ أَعْلَمُ بِإِيمَـٰنِهِنَّ ۖ فَإِنْ عَلِمْتُمُوهُنَّ
مُؤْمِنَـٰتٍ فَلَا تَرْجِعُوهُنَّ إِلَى ٱلْكُفَّارِ ۖ لَا هُنَّ حِلٌّ لَّهُمْ
وَلَا هُمْ يَحِلُّونَ لَهُنَّ ۖ وَءَاتُوهُم مَّآ أَنفَقُوا۟ ۚ وَلَا جُنَاحَ
عَلَيْكُمْ أَن تَنكِحُوهُنَّ إِذَآ ءَاتَيْتُمُوهُنَّ أُجُورَهُنَّ ۚ وَلَا
تُمْسِكُوا۟ بِعِصَمِ ٱلْكَوَافِرِ وَسْـَٔلُوا۟ مَآ أَنفَقْتُمْ وَلْيَسْـَٔلُوا۟ مَآ

أَنفَقُواْ ۚ ذَٰلِكُمْ حُكْمُ ٱللَّهِ ۖ يَحْكُمُ بَيْنَكُمْ ۚ وَٱللَّهُ عَلِيمٌ حَكِيمٌ ﴿١٠﴾

They are not lawful (wives) for the disbelievers nor are the Disbelievers lawful (husbands) for them. [*Al-Mumtahinah*:10].

Also, the Prophet ﷺ said: "(The distinction) between man and polytheism and *Kufr* is abandoning of prayer", reported by *Tirmidhi*, *Nasaai* and others. In addition, the insult of the *deen* is considered by all Muslims to be a major *Kufr*. Therefore, you are obliged to hate him for the sake of Allah and be separated from him, Allah ﷻ says:

وَمَن يَتَّقِ ٱللَّهَ يَجْعَل لَّهُۥ مَخْرَجًا ﴿٢﴾ وَيَرْزُقْهُ مِنْ حَيْثُ لَا يَحْتَسِبُ ۚ وَمَن يَتَوَكَّلْ عَلَى ٱللَّهِ فَهُوَ حَسْبُهُۥٓ ۚ إِنَّ ٱللَّهَ بَٰلِغُ أَمْرِهِۦ ۚ قَدْ جَعَلَ ٱللَّهُ لِكُلِّ شَىْءٍ قَدْرًا ﴿٣﴾

And whoever fears Allah and keeps his duty to Him, He will make a way for him to get out from every difficulty. And He will provide him from (sources) he never could imagine. [*At-Talaaq*:2-3].

I call upon Allah ﷻ to help you in your problem and save

you from your husband's misdeeds, and to guide him to the right path and grant him repentance, He is the Most Generous.

Winning the
Heart of your
Husband
خير نسائكم الولود الودود
Ibraahim ibn Saaleh al-Mahmud

The Exuberant Husband

Aisha ﷺ narrated that Allah's messenger ﷺ said: "I know when you are pleased with me or angry with me." I said, "How do you know that?" He said: "When you are pleased with me, you say, "No, by the Lord of Muhammad, but when you are angry with me, then you say, no, by the Lord of Ibrahim". Thereupon, I said: "Yes, you are right, by Allah, O Allah's messenger, I leave nothing but your name."[15] She also reported that she was with Allah's messenger during a journey. She said, "I was not bulky, he told his companion to move forward and they did. He then told me: "come and race me". I raced him on foot and I beat him. But, on another journey, when I became bulky, he asked me to race him. I raced him and he beat me. He started laughing and said: "This makes up for that beating"[16]

In this race, the Prophet ﷺ intends to teach the married couple how to enjoy each other's company. They could perform some innocent activities and entertainment together so that they would not feel bored. Aisha ﷺ said: "I stained the face of Suwayda and Suwayda stained the face of Aisha, and the Prophet ﷺ started laughing". "The Prophet ﷺ used

[15] Agreed upon

[16] Reported by *Ahmad*, *Abu Daawud* and others.

to wash himself together with one of his wives from the same vessel"[17]

[17] Reported by *Al-Bukhaari*.

Important Questions

Question 1: Sheikh al-Islam Ahmad Ibnu Taymiyya was asked about a woman who does not pray, should her husband order her to pray?, If she does not want to, should he leave her or not?

Answer 1: Yes, the husband should order his wife to pray, and he even has to order other people if he can because Allah ﷻ said:

وَأْمُرْ أَهْلَكَ بِٱلصَّلَوٰةِ وَٱصْطَبِرْ عَلَيْهَا ۖ لَا نَسْـَٔلُكَ رِزْقًا ۖ نَّحْنُ نَرْزُقُكَ ۗ وَٱلْعَـٰقِبَةُ لِلتَّقْوَىٰ ﴿١٣٢﴾

"And enjoin prayer on your family, and be patient in offering them (the prayers)". [*Taaha*: 132],

And

يَـٰٓأَيُّهَا ٱلَّذِينَ ءَامَنُوا۟ قُوٓا۟ أَنفُسَكُمْ وَأَهْلِيكُمْ نَارًا وَقُودُهَا ٱلنَّاسُ وَٱلْحِجَارَةُ عَلَيْهَا مَلَـٰٓئِكَةٌ غِلَاظٌ شِدَادٌ لَّا يَعْصُونَ ٱللَّهَ مَآ أَمَرَهُمْ وَيَفْعَلُونَ مَا يُؤْمَرُونَ ﴿٦﴾

"O you who believe! Ward off from yourselves and

your family a fire whose fuel is men and stones". [*At-Tahreem*:6].

The Prophet ﷺ said: "Teach them and punish them". However, the husband has to induce her to pray by asking her kindly; but if she refuses to do so, he has to divorce her, because anyone who abandons prayers deserves punishment as agreed by all Muslims. He even has to be killed if he persists in abandoning prayers, for he is considered a *Kafir* (disbeliever) and apostate according to two famous accounts and Allah knows best.

Question 2: Sheikh al-Islam Ibnu Taymiyya was asked about a man who took his wife to live in a place full of filthy people and often took her outside and meet indecent people. If anybody asked him to move from this house, he would say: I am her husband, her master and the master of the house. Did he have the right to do so?

Answer 2: All praise be to Allah, the Lord of the world, this man has no right to force his wife to live wherever he likes, nor take her and mix with sinners and evil-doers. Instead, he has to find her a decent and nice place that suits her, and keep away from wicked people, and if not, he has to be punished twice: one for the sins he committed and one for not safeguarding his wife's honour and for taking her to corrupt places. This punishment will prevent him and anybody who may try to do the same thing for his wife. And Allah knows best.

Question 3: Although my husband, may Allah forgive him, is endowed with noble character and fear of Allah, but he does not care about me at all in the house. He is always angry and annoyed. You might say I am responsible for that; but, Allah ﷻ knows that I fulfill all my duties towards him, always endeavour to provide all means of peace and rest and endure his misbehaviour. However, whenever I ask him about anything or talk to him about a matter, he becomes irritated and shouted: this is stupid and silly, whereas when he is with his friends, he becomes happy and cheerful. As for me, I only receive reprimands and ill-treatment, and feel tormented and sad; more than that, I often think of leaving the house.

I have little education but I do all my obligations assigned by Allah.

His Eminence the Sheikh, Do I sin If I leave the house and bring up my children and bear the responsibility of life alone? Or shall I stay with him in this situation and not bother to talk to him and share his feelings and problems?

Help me, what shall I do? May Allah bless you.

Answer 3: Without doubt, it is obligatory for the married couple to live honourably and to share mutual love and noble character for Allah ﷻ says:

يَٰٓأَيُّهَا ٱلَّذِينَ ءَامَنُواْ لَا يَحِلُّ لَكُمْ أَن تَرِثُواْ ٱلنِّسَآءَ كَرْهًا ۖ وَلَا تَعْضُلُوهُنَّ لِتَذْهَبُواْ بِبَعْضِ مَآ ءَاتَيْتُمُوهُنَّ إِلَّآ أَن يَأْتِينَ بِفَٰحِشَةٍ مُّبَيِّنَةٍ ۚ وَعَاشِرُوهُنَّ بِٱلْمَعْرُوفِ ۚ فَإِن كَرِهْتُمُوهُنَّ فَعَسَىٰٓ أَن تَكْرَهُواْ شَيْـًٔا وَيَجْعَلَ ٱللَّهُ فِيهِ خَيْرًا كَثِيرًا ﴿١٩﴾

And live with them honourably. [*An-Nsaa*:19]

and also

وَٱلْمُطَلَّقَٰتُ يَتَرَبَّصْنَ بِأَنفُسِهِنَّ ثَلَٰثَةَ قُرُوٓءٍ ۚ وَلَا
يَحِلُّ لَهُنَّ أَن يَكْتُمْنَ مَا خَلَقَ ٱللَّهُ فِىٓ أَرْحَامِهِنَّ إِن كُنَّ
يُؤْمِنَّ بِٱللَّهِ وَٱلْيَوْمِ ٱلْءَاخِرِ ۚ وَبُعُولَتُهُنَّ أَحَقُّ بِرَدِّهِنَّ فِى
ذَٰلِكَ إِنْ أَرَادُوٓا۟ إِصْلَٰحًا ۚ وَلَهُنَّ مِثْلُ ٱلَّذِى عَلَيْهِنَّ
بِٱلْمَعْرُوفِ ۚ وَلِلرِّجَالِ عَلَيْهِنَّ دَرَجَةٌ ۗ وَٱللَّهُ عَزِيزٌ حَكِيمٌ

And they, women, have rights over their husbands as regards living expenses, etc. similar to those of their husbands over them as regards obedience and respect, etc. to what is reasonable. [*Al-Baqarah*:228]

The Prophet ﷺ said: "Righteousness is the most noble character", reported by *Muslim*; also, the Prophet ﷺ said: "The most perfect of the believers in faith is he who is most excellent of them in morals and the best of you are they who are best of you to their wives, and I am best of you to my household", reported by *Muslim*. There are many more hadith that indicate the necessity for noble character, good conduct and behaviour between Muslims in general and between married couples and relatives in particular.

You have been excellent by patiently bearing your husband's misbehaviour and ill-treatment. But, I advise you to be more patient and not to leave the house and If Allah wills you will be rewarded for your patience because Allah ﷻ says:

وَأَطِيعُوا۟ ٱللَّهَ وَرَسُولَهُۥ وَلَا تَنَٰزَعُوا۟ فَتَفْشَلُوا۟ وَتَذْهَبَ رِيحُكُمْ ۖ وَٱصْبِرُوٓا۟ ۚ إِنَّ ٱللَّهَ مَعَ ٱلصَّٰبِرِينَ ﴿٤٦﴾

and be patient. Surely, Allah is with those who are patient. [*Al-Anfaal*:46]

And

قَالُوٓا۟ أَءِنَّكَ لَأَنتَ يُوسُفُ ۖ قَالَ أَنَا۠ يُوسُفُ وَهَٰذَآ أَخِى ۖ قَدْ مَنَّ ٱللَّهُ عَلَيْنَآ ۖ إِنَّهُۥ مَن يَتَّقِ وَيَصْبِرْ فَإِنَّ ٱللَّهَ لَا يُضِيعُ أَجْرَ ٱلْمُحْسِنِينَ ﴿٩٠﴾

Verily, he who fears Allah with obedience to Him, by abstaining from sins and evil deeds, and by performing righteous good deeds, and is patient, then surely, Allah makes not the reward of the good-doers to be lost. [*Yusuf*:90]

And

قُلْ يَٰعِبَادِ ٱلَّذِينَ ءَامَنُوا۟ ٱتَّقُوا۟ رَبَّكُمْ ۚ لِلَّذِينَ أَحْسَنُوا۟ فِى هَٰذِهِ ٱلدُّنْيَا حَسَنَةٌ ۗ وَأَرْضُ ٱللَّهِ وَٰسِعَةٌ ۗ إِنَّمَا يُوَفَّى ٱلصَّٰبِرُونَ أَجْرَهُم بِغَيْرِ حِسَابٍ ﴿١٠﴾

Only those who are patient shall receive their rewards in full without reckoning. [*Az-zumar*:10]

And

تِلْكَ مِنْ أَنۢبَآءِ ٱلْغَيْبِ نُوحِيهَآ إِلَيْكَ ۖ مَا كُنتَ تَعْلَمُهَآ أَنتَ وَلَا قَوْمُكَ مِن قَبْلِ هَٰذَا ۖ فَٱصْبِرْ ۖ إِنَّ ٱلْعَٰقِبَةَ لِلْمُتَّقِينَ ﴿٤٩﴾

So, be patient. Surely, the good end is for the pious and righteous persons. [*Hud*:49]

Hence, there is no harm in playing with him and in your conversation try to be gentle and use words that will soften his heart, make him feel happy and observe your rights over him. In addition, do not ask him about worldly needs as long as he fulfils essential duties, and afterwards, when he is delighted he will carry out all your requirements.

I call upon Allah to help you succeed in reforming your

husband's conduct and behaviour, to help him come to his senses and to bestow upon him noble character, cheerfulness and to respect your rights. He is the most Answerable and the Guide.

Question 4: My husband often gets angry for silly reason, and I can not bear his anger, so I retaliate. Unfortunately, he becomes more angry and furious, and it results in an argument between us which could last for hours.

Answer 4: Sister, you are not the only one who is suffering from this problem, but a lot of wives feel the same, particularly in this era where man faces many problems at work every day and suppress them till he comes home where he takes out his anger and frustration on his wife's and children's faces for silly reason. What I am saying is not a justification for the husband's actions, but only an explanation to the angry state that descend unexpectedly upon the poor wife. Therefore, the solution, which I think, is that the wife should not meet her husband with the same furious temper. Instead, she could tell him: "Allah forgive you". However, even this action might not restrain his anger; but, you have to be more patient and remain firm and use other apologies like "I am to blame", "I have been negligent" and so on. Consequently, minutes will pass and at the most half an hour, then your husband will become composed and remember his enraged state and your composure towards his bad temper. He will feel ashamed and respect you, and your marriage will be safe after these tense and uneasy moments.

Wahid Abdussalam Bali

A husband threatens with divorce!!!

- He threatens his wife with divorce for silly things!!
- He threatens with divorce if there is a simple misunderstanding!!
- He threatens with divorce if the children cry!!
- He threatens with divorce if the children break a glass or a cup!!
- He threatened with divorce if his wife forgets to bring his shirt!!

This is one of the funniest and rare stories about the people who threaten with divorce.

In one of their conversations, a man told Arrasheed, Commander of the Faithful: I was informed that an Arab had divorced five women in one day. Arrasheed then said: A man can only have four women, how come he has five?. The man said: There was an Arab who had four women. One day he came home and found them arguing, and he was ill-natured, he told himself: How long will this dispute go on? He told one of his four wives "you are the one responsible for this dispute" and he divorces her. Her friend told him: "you have unfairly divorced her, if you punished her otherwise, you would have been just with her". He then told her: "you are also divorced". The third one told him: Shame on you, by Allah they were both nice to you and better than you, but he told her: " You too, who enumerate their merits, are divorced. The fourth wife said angrily: " You are unable to discipline your wives, you can only divorce them". He then told her: "You are divorced as well".

This incident took place within earshot of his neighbour, she came to him and said: "By Allah, the Arabs could only confirm your weakness and the weakness of your people when they experience your conduct and behaviour, you insisted on divorcing all your four wives in one hour. He said: "You are also divorced if your husband allows me", her husband replied from within the house: "Yes, I agree, I agree".

Wise brother:

Do not allow your house to be reigned by anxiety and distress.

Do not threaten your wife with divorce for silly reasons.

Make your life full of love, harmony, understanding and respect and take a lesson from the aforementioned story.

What is worth mentioning is the problem of swearing to divorce one's wife which has prevailed among many Muslims. For silly reasons, some men will swear to divorce their wives, and this problem should be avoided because some Muslim scholars conclude that it is an irrevocable divorce.

A wife pleading with her husband not to travel!

When the husband travels away, his wife remains anxious. What can she do? How can she manage? She falls into a critical situation with her family, and feels ashamed of her children! She fights the ardour of love and swallows bitterness. What can she tell the children when they ask about their father? Can she lie to them? Can she deceive herself? She is embarrassed, worried and miserable!

"Do not ask me about him, he has flown away"

"He left and set fire to my heart"

"Do not ask me about him, I feel grief inside and the sadness in my heart is deep"

"Do not ask me about him when he says farewell

I sensed in his words deception and secrets"

"He left and in the children's eyes questions

Which I answer with lies and excuses"

"He left to sleep in another woman's arms, in whose warmth he will forget the children and the house"

To all husbands:

Fear Allah with regard to your wives. Protect them and give them their rights that Allah has given them.

For you brother, I write this story about a man who abandons what is *Halal* (legal and allowed) and seeks *Haram* (forbidden). He left behind virtue and run after depravity.

There was a married man who had children; but, unfortunately, he was still immersed in his old bad habit. He thought only about his pleasure and desire, be it *Halal* or *Haram*. He travelled from his country to another one in Eastern Asia, and he was still young and full of life. In one of his evening parties, he met a prostitute dancer who took him to her room. No sooner had he touched her than the decisive moment came, the Angel of Death was waiting for him. The Angel of Death took his soul and the dead man was returned to his country in his coffin.

I ask Allah ﷻ safety and good health.

Conclusion

My brother, the husband:

At the end of this message, I would like to mention to you some advice which, if you follow, you will, if Allah wills, live with your wife in happiness and harmony:

1- Religion is sincerity

2- The most perfect of the believers in faith is he who is most excellent of them in morals and the best of you are they who are best of you to their wives,

3- Beware of avarice

4- Whatever you spend on your wife intending to receive Allah's reward is regarded as *Sadaqa* (Act of charity).

5- Nobody should be informed about your marriage problems.

6- Do not use obscene language with your wife's relatives.

7- Do not insult your wife.

8- Always smile in front of your wife.

9- Love each other and be calm.

10- Educate your children according to Islamic teachings.

11- Minimize your visits to markets.

12- Avoid buying clothes with pictures.

13- Do not buy indecent clothes for your daughters.

14- Organize an Islamic session with your family at home.

15- Be gentle with your wife and children.

16- Do not beat your wife without reason.

17- Adorn yourself for your wife.

Is there any reward for good other than good?

Muslim Brother:

To gain your wife's heart does not mean to give up your rights or to relinquish your guardianship. Because, unfortunately, a lot of people are either extreme or negligent in dealing with the subject of guardianship. For example, if some men want to buy a car, furniture, change the colour of the house or some clothes, they let their wives alone choose the colour and the form. Other men are firm and will not seek their wives opinion at all. However, the best of affairs is to follow a course middle, we are a middle *Ummah* in everything.

I call upon Allah ﷻ to grant all Muslims happiness in this world and in the Hereafter. He is the Guide to the straight path.

A Message from the Publishers

Dear Brothers, whoever amongst you wishes to gain peace, happiness and success for himself and his family, in both this life and the hereafter should seek to follow the example of the best of generations, the companions of the Prophet ﷺ in their practice of Islam and their rememberance of Allah.

To this end, *Al-Firdous* here presents some authentic stories of the Companions of the Prophet and the pious predecessors.

PURIFICATION
DOCTRINES
SALAT
ZAKAT
SIYAM
HAJJ
FIQH
OF WORSHIP
فقه
العبادات
Sheikh Muhammad Salih Ibn al-'Uthaymeen

Stories from the Predecessors[18]

A man went to Ibrahim ibn Adliani ﷺ and said: 'O Abu Ishaq I transgress against myself (by committing sins). Inform me of a deterrent that will deliver my heart.' Ibrahim ﷺ said: 'If you accept five practices and remain steadfast on them, nothing will harm and no (sinful) pleasure will destroy you:

1. If you want to disobey Allah, then do not eat from His provisions. How can you bite the hands that feed you?

2. If you want to disobey Allah, then do not live in a place that He owns. How can you eat and live off someone you wish to disobey?

3. And if you (are such an ingrate) and still wish to disobey Him, then find a place where you can do so inconspicuously. How can you (have the audacity to) commit a sin when He is always Present in front of you?

4. When the Angel of Death arrives, ask him to delay taking your soul for a while so that you are able to

[18] This Chapter is taken from Chapter 9 of *Sincere Repentance* Al-Firdous Ltd, 1995

make a sincere repentance and perform some good deeds for Allah. The angel will not grant you your desire and will immediately dispatch your soul to the next world. How can you expect to escape?

5. When the angels of Hell come to escort you to Hell, don't follow them. You will not be able to resist so how do you expect to save yourself'

The man said: 'Enough, enough Ibrahim. I will make a sincere repentance right now.' The man did so and stayed with Ibrahim ﵀ until death separated them.[19]

Fudail ibn 'Ayad ﵀ used to be a highway robber and was madly in love with a young woman. One night as he was scaling the walls of the young woman's house, he heard someone reciting the following verse of Surah Hadeed (57:16):

'Is it not time for believers to subject their hearts to the remembrance of Allah...'

Fudail was so taken in by the verse that he immediately repented and spent the night in a derelict place nearby. Later in the night, he heard a few travellers shout: "Beware, beware! Fudail is ahead of you. He will rob you!" Fudail shouted: 'Fudail has repented!' He promised

---

[19] Muwaqif Mushriqah Fi Hayatis Salaf: 15

the travellers safe passage. Fudail ibn'Ayad ﷺ became a beacon of guidance and his sayings are still quoted today.[20]

◇◇◇◇◇◇◇◇◇

A nightmare that prompted the repentance of a great sage:

Malik ibn Dinar ﷺ was asked about the reason behind his repentance. He said: I used to be a policeman and an alcoholic. I then acquired a maid who was very good to me. She bore a daughter of ours to whom I became very attached. I became even more fond of her when she started to crawl. Whenever I used to serve myself wine, she would come and drag my tumbler away from me and spill everything over my clothes. Our daughter died when she turned two and I was devastated.

The 15th of Sha'ban came along that year on a Friday. I went to sleep drunk and without offering my prayers. I saw in a dream that the Day of Judgement had come about: the Trumpet was blown; graves were resurrected and people were being gathered and I was among them. I heard a hissing noise behind. I turned around and saw that I was being approached by a huge black and blue snake. I started to run away as fast as I could trembling with fear.

I then encountered an old man who was well dressed and wore good perfume. I greeted him and asked him to help

---

[20] Ibid: 24

me. The old man cried and said that he was very weak and the snake was much stronger than he. However, he did tell me to keep on running in the hope that I would find something that would save me from the snake.

I continued to run and climbed on top of an elevated area. I found myself on top of a valley of fire. The horror of the fire alone made me almost fall into it. Then, I heard someone shouting: 'Get away from there. You don't belong there.' I found security in that shout and ran further with the snake still at my heels. I found the old man again and pleaded with him to help. Again, he started to cry and say that he was very weak and that the snake was far stronger than he. Then, the old man directed me towards a hill where he said I might find a deposit of mine that could help me.

I looked at the hill which was circular and made of silver. In the hill were pierced windows and hanging curtains. Every window had two golden panels and each panel was adorned with silk curtains. I quickly ran towards the hill. An angel then cried: 'Raise the curtains. Open the panels and look. Perhaps this afflicted person has some sort of deposit here that can help him.' I then saw faces of small children who were like small moons peeping out from the windows. Then one of them shouted: 'What's wrong with you all. Come quickly. His enemy has almost come upon him.'

So they came and looked from their windows - hundreds of them. Then, I saw the face of my daughter who had died. When she saw me, she cried and said: 'By Allah! That is my father.' She then shot out of the window like an arrow from a bow and jumped into a pool of light (noor). She then appeared in front of me and extended one of her hands to me. I grabbed and hung on to her. She put her other hand in front of the snake and drove it away. She then made me sit down and sat herself in my lap, stroked her right hand through my beard and said: "O father: 'Is it not time for believers to subject their hearts to the remembrance of Allah.'"

I started to cry and asked how she knew the Quran. She said they (the children) knew more than they (in the world) did. I then asked her about the snake that ran after me. She explained that it represented my bad deeds which would drive me into Hell. I then enquired about the old man. She said he was my good deeds which had become so weak that they were unable to defend me against my bad deeds. I then asked what they were doing inside this hill. She informed me that they were the deceased children of Muslims waiting for their parents to join them. They would intercede for their parents on the Day of Judgement.

Malik said: 'I woke up in fright. I smashed all my wine containers and repented. This was how I repented.'[21]

The very same Malik ibn Dinar ﷺ says that he was once walking through an alley of Basra when he saw a beautiful regal maid riding and being escorted by several servants. Malik called out to her and said: '0 maid! Will your

---

[21] Ibid: 49

master sell you?'

'How can you say that old man?' she replied.

'Will your master sell you?' Malik asked again.

'If he does, are the likes of you going to buy?' she asked.

'Yes! Even better than you.'

She laughed and asked her servants to escort Malik to her quarters. On arriving at her place, the maid informed her master who also laughed and asked to see Malik. Malik was brought in and had an immediate impact on the master.

'What do you want?' the master asked him.

'Sell me your maid,' Malik said.

'Can you afford to buy her?'

'To me she is worth no more than two rotten date pits.'

Everybody in the room burst into laughter.

'How can her price be that,' they all asked mockingly.

'Because she has so many defects,' Malik retorted.

'And just what might her defects be?'

'If she does not wear perfume her perspiration stinks,' said Malik.

'If she does not brush her teeth, her teeth give off foul odour. If she does not groom her hair, it becomes infested with lice and disheveled. If she lives for a few more years, she will become an old woman. She menstruates, urinates and defecates. Perhaps she only likes you for selfish reasons. She probably isn't loyal to you and if you die before her, she will find someone else just like you.

I am in a position to buy - for much cheaper than what you want for your maid - a maid whose constitution is of pure camphor: if she were to mix her expectorate in salty, bitter water, it would become sweet; if she were to speak to the dead, they would respond (to the melody of her voice). If she raised her hand toward the sun, it would lose it shine; if she appeared at night, it would radiate with light and if she confronted the horizon with her dresses and jewellery, she would adorn it (the horizon). She is a maid who has been nurtured in musk and saffron; raised in gardens and suckled by the waters of Tasneem (Waters of Paradise). She will never be disloyal and her love for you will never falter. Which one of these maids is more deserving of a price?' Malik concluded.

'The one you described,' the master conceded.

'Then you should know that she is very affordable and accessible.'

'What is her price? May Allah have mercy on you.'

'Very cheap. Spare a moment at night and offer two units of prayer with sincerity. When you place food in front of you, think of the hungry and sacrifice your craving for lavish food (and feed the hungry). Remove stones (impediments) and dirt (obstacles) from the road. Spend the remainder of your life on bare necessities. Remove your worries of this world of oblivion so that you may live in this world with the honour of an abstemious person, go tomorrow to the station of dignity in peace and dwell in Paradise for ever.'

The master turned to the maid and asked: '0 maid! Have you listened to what our old man has said?'

'Yes,' she replied.

'Has he spoken the truth, or is he merely telling a tale?'

'No he has spoken the truth. He has been kind and offered advice.'

The master then exclaimed: 'If that is the case, then you are free for the sake of Allah. And such and such property is yours. And all you servants around me, you are all free and you may have such and such properties. This house of mine and everything in it is a charity in the path of Allah.'

He then ripped a piece of rough curtain cloth and replaced his expensive clothes with the curtain cloth. The maid remarked: 'I have no life after you, my master. She also took off her attire and replaced it with some rough clothing and set off with her master. Malik saw them off: he took one route and they took another.[22]

Sulaiman ibn Khalid says that a young maid of an old lady

---

[22] Kitabul Taibeen Minal Mubook Was Salateen: 14

was mentioned to Hisham ibn Abdul Malik (the Khalifah in Damascus 105 All). This young girl was renowned for her beauty, good manners, recitation of the Quran and prolific poetry. Hisham sent orders by post to the governor of Kufa to have the girl bought for whatever her owner (the old lady) asked for and then to have her immediately. sent to him. He sent along a servant for her.

When the governor received the letter, he sent for the old lady who sold the girl for 2,000 dirhams and a date orchard which would yield five hundred mithqal (a unit of weight) of dates every year. The governor dressed the girl in royal clothing and sent her to Hisham. Hisham gave her own quarters and an escort of servants, presented her with some precious jewels and extravagant clothing.

One day while Hisham was with her on a luxurious balcony which was enhanced with cushions and perfume, she related some intriguing stories to him and composed some poems. Suddenly, there were cries for help. Hisham looked over the balcony and saw a hearse accompanied by people. Behind the procession was a group of mourning women. One mourner cried out aloud:

'O you who are being carried on wooden sticks; you who are being taken to the dead; you who are about to be left alone in your grave and you who are about to be made a stranger in your resting place. O you who are being transferred. If only I knew whether you are telling those who are carrying you to hurry up. or whether you are asking them where they are taking you and to take you back.'

Hisham started to weep, discarded his pleasure and started to say: 'Death is admonition enough.'

Ghadid (the girl) said: 'This mourner has broken my heart.'

Hisham said: 'it is a very serious matter' and called the servant. He came down from the balcony and left. Ghadid remained stuck to her couch. That night she dreamt that someone came to her and said:

'You are flattered by your beauty and you lure with your charm. How will you be when the trumpet is blown (on the Day of Judgement); when people are resurrected and then confronted with their actions.' Ghadid woke frightened and drank something to pacify herself. She then called upon one of her servants and asked her to prepare a bath for her. After her bath, she got rid of her jewels and clothes and wore a woollen jalabiyah and tied a string around her waist. She took a cane with a bag over it and stormed into Hishani's room. Hisham did not recognise her. 'I am Ghadid, your girl,' she said. 'A warner came to me and his warning shook me. You have had your pleasure with me. I have come to ask you to free me from the slavery of this world.'

'There is so much difference between those who seek pleasure. You are with your pleasure, so go you are free for the sake of Allah. But where do you intend to go?' Hisham enquired.

'I want to visit the House of Allah,' replied she.

'Go,' replied Hisham. 'No one will be in your way.'

She left the capital and arrived in Makkah where she remained in fasting during the day like a gazelle in its den. When night came she would perform tawaf of the Ka'bah and say:

‘O my treasure you are my provision. Don’t cut off my hope; grant me my wish; make good my return and be generous in giving me reward.’ She became very famous and died worshipping. May Allah have mercy upon her.[23]

Ibrahim ibn Bashshar, the protégé of Ibrahim ibn Adham ﷺ says that he asked Ibrahim about the beginning of his quest to serve Allah. Ibrahim said:

‘My father was a king of Balkh (Central Khurasan). We used to love hunting. I went out one day on my horse accompanied by my dog. Suddenly a rabbit or a fox jumped up and agitated my horse. Then, I heard a voice from behind me saying:

“You have not been created for this; nor have you been ordered to do this (hunting for pleasure).”

I looked around me to the left and right but I did not see anybody. I cursed the Devil and continued to ride. But then, my horse started to shake again and I heard the same voice saying the same thing. I looked around and found no one so I cursed the devil again and tried to continue. But my horse would not stop trying to shake me off. Then, I heard a voice from beneath my saddle bow calling me by my name and saying:

[23] Ibid: 22

“O Ibrahim! You have not been created for this; nor have you been ordered to do this.”

So I stopped and realised that a warner from the Lord of the Worlds had come to wake me up from my state of oblivion. I vowed not to disobey my Lord from this day, lest He does not protect me. Then I returned to my family. I went to see one of my father’s shepherds and exchanged my clothes for his long shirt and a blanket. Then I travelled across the mountains and valleys to Iraq.

I worked there for a few days but I was not satisfied with the purity of my earnings. I asked a learned person about this and he told me to go to Syria. I did so and reached a town called Al-Mansoora (or Maseesah). But even here, I was not satisfied with the purity of my earnings. Another learned person told me to go to Tarsoos where there was said to be plenty of work and good pure earnings. I went there and sat on the beach when a man came and hired me to be a warden for his orchards.

I remained as a rural warden many days until one day a servant came along with many friends and shouted: “0 warden!”. I went over to him. He asked me to bring them the biggest and best pomegranate. I went and brought him the biggest pomegranate. He cut it and found it very sour and complained: “Warden! You have been here been in our orchard for so many days eating our fruits, but yet you don’t know the difference between a good pomegranate and a sour one?” I told him I had never tasted any of the fruits I guarded. The servant pointed towards his companions and said: “Did you hear what he said? He couldn’t have said anything more if he were Ibrahim ibn Adham.”

The servant left and discussed me in the masjid the next day. One person recognised who I was. The servant came to the orchard with a large contingent of people. I hid amongst the trees and scampered as soon as I had the chance to do so. This was the beginning of my quest and this is how I left Tarsoos to travel the desert.'[24]

Abdullah ibn Faraj رضي الله عنه says that he was in need of a handyman for his house whom he could pay daily. So he went to the bazaar and found a pale young boy wearing a woolen shirt tied with a woolen belt and had a big basket and a rope in his hands. Abdullah asked him if he would be willing to work. The boy said yes and asked to be paid one dirham and one daniq (1/6th of a dirham). The boy also stipulated that he would discontinue work and prepare for prayers when the adhan of Zuhr was given and likewise at the time of Asr.

Abdullah agreed and took him to his house where he showed him what he had to do. The boy worked well with his hands and did not speak until the adhan for Zuhr was given. He reminded Abdullah of the condition. Abdullah told him to leave. The boy went offered his prayers and came back to work until Asr. The boy went for Asr, came

---

[24] Ibid: 29

back and worked until the end of the day. The boy left when Abdullah gave him wages.

After a few days, Abdullah needed some work done again. His wife told him to find the very same boy because he was good and honest. Abdullah went in search of the boy but could not find him. On enquiring, people told him that he only worked on Saturdays and that he was a loner. Abdullah waited for Saturday to come and found the boy. The boy agreed to work on the same conditions. At the end of the day's work, Abdullah offered the boy extra wages. The boy was very displeased and left. Abdullah ran after him and begged him to take at least what he had asked for. He did so and left.

Some time later, Abdullah needed to hire the boy again. He waited for Saturday to come and went to the bazaar. He did not find the boy there. Someone told him that the boy spent one daniq every day but had been taken ill. Abdullah found out where he lived and went to visit him. He was staying in the house of an old woman. He found the boy sleeping with his head resting on a brick. 'Do you need anything,' asked Abdullah.

'Yes,' replied the boy, 'if you accept.'

Abdullah said he would.

'When I die,' the boy continued, 'sell my rope, wash my shirt and belt and then bury me in them. Look inside the pocket of my shirt. There is a ring in it. Wait until the day Harun-al-Rashid (the Khalifah at the time) comes to town. Stand in a place where he can see you and then approach him and show him the ring. But do this after you have buried me.' Abdullah agreed to do so.

When the boy died, Abdullah did as the boy requested. When Harun-al-Rashid came to town, he went to see him, informed him that he had a trust for him and waved the ring. Harun summoned Abdullah to his quarters. When Abdullah went, Harun excused everybody from his presence and asked Abdullah who he was and where he got the ring from. Abdullah answered both questions. Harun heard the long story of the boy and wept so much that Abdullah started to feel sorry for him. 'O leader of the believers!' Abdullah addressed the Khalifa. 'Who was this boy to you?' 'He was my son!' the Khalifah exclaimed.

'How did he become like that?'

'He was born before I became entrusted with the Khilafah. He was brought up very well and was well educated in the Quran and other sciences. When I assumed the Khilafah, he left and did not care for any of my worldly belongings. He was very fond of his mother so I gave her this expensive sapphire ring to give to him. He took the ring very reluctantly. His mother since passed away and you are the only person who has informed me of him. You will take me to his grave tonight.'

Abdullah took Harun to his son's grave. Harun wept for a long time and remained there until dawn. Harun asked Abdullah to stay with him a few days so that he could visit the grave at nights. Abdullah did not know that the boy was the son of Harun until Harun himself told him.[25]

---

[25] Ibid: 37

by

Dr. Naahah Ibrahim, Asim Abdul Maajid
& Esaam-ud-Deen Darbaalah

How The Companions Feared Allah[26]

Abu Imraan Al-Juni ﵁ reports that Abu Bakr Siddiq ﵁ used to say: 'I wish I was a hair in the side of a believer.'[27]

Hasan ﵁ narrates that Abu Bakr ﵁ used to say: 'If only I were a tree cut down and eaten.'[28]

Abdullah ibn Omar ﵁ says that Omar ﵁ used to say: 'If a goat had died with the driftage of the Euphrates, I would worry that Omar might be held accountable for it.'[29]

Abdullah ibn Amir says that he saw Omar ﵁ pick up a piece of grass and remark: 'If only I were this piece of grass; if only I was not created; if only my mother had not given birth to me; if only I were naught and if only I could become completely forgotten.[30]

Abdullah ibn Isa ﵁ says that Omar ﵁ had two black

---

[26] This Chapter is taken from Chapter 3 of *Fear of Allah* Al-Firdous Ltd, 1995

[27] Sifatus Safwah: *1/251*

[28] Ibid

[29] Ibid: 1/275; it has also been quoted in Hilya and Ihya in a different version.

[30] Ibid

streaks on his face because of constant weeping[31]

Omar ﷺ also used to say: 'If someone announced from the heavens that everybody will enter Paradise except one person, I would fear that that person would be me.'[32]

Abdullah ibn Abbas ﷺ said to Omar ﷺ when he was stabbed: 'O Leader of the Believers! You accepted Islam others disbelieved; you struggled along with the Prophet ﷺ when others deserted him; the Prophet ﷺ died while he was pleased with you; no two people have disagreed with you and you are about to die as a martyr.' Omar ﷺ replied: 'The flattered is the one whom you flatter. By Allah! If I had what ever the sun rose upon I would give it away in order to protect myself from what is about to rise (upon me).'[33]

It is narrated from Abu Maisarah ﷺ that whenever he went to bed he would say: 'If only my mother had not given birth to me.' His wife once asked him why he kept on saying that especially when Allah had favoured him and granted him Islam. He said: 'That is true. But he has also informed us that we will approach the fire without informing us whether or not we will come out from it. (Referring to verse 71/72 in Surah Maryam.)

Abdullah ibn Masood ﷺ says: 'It is important for the one who memorises the Quran that he should recognise his nights when people are asleep; his days when people are not fasting; his grief when people are content; his weeping

---

[31] Ibid

[32] Takhweef: 13

[33] Tanbeehul Ghafileen: 2/418

when people laugh (in indifference); his silence when they talk and his humbleness when they are proud.'

'A bearer of the Quran should be concerned, tolerant, tranquil and lenient. He should not be uncouth, oblivious, a loud mouth nor a difficult person.'[34]

Ibn Abbas ﷺ was asked about those who fear. He said: 'Their hearts are pleased with fear; their eyes weep; they say: 'How can we be content when death is behind us and the grave is in front of us; judgement is our promised (time); Hell is on our way and we have to face our Lord?'[35]

Masrooq ﷺ says a man was with Abdullah ibn Masood ﷺ and said: 'I do not wish to be among the People of The Right Hand (a station mentioned in Surah Waqi'ah). I would prefer to be among the Ones given Proximity (another station).' Abdullah ﷺ said: 'There is a person here who would prefer that he not be resurrected at all (himself).'[36]

Abu Wa-il ﷺ says that Abdullah used to say: 'I would like that Allah forgives one of my sins and not mention my genealogy.'[37]

Harith ibn Suwaid ﷺ says 'If you knew what I know about

---

[34] Ibid: 2/6 18

[35] Ihya: 4/181

[36] Sifatus Safwah: 1/405

[37] Ibid

myself, you would throw dirt over me.'[38]

Once, Abdullah ibn Rawah cried in front of his wife so she cried too. 'Why are you crying?' He asked her. 'Because you were crying,' she replied. He explained that he was crying because Allah had informed him that he would approach Hell, but did not inform him of coming out of there.[39]

Thaur ibn Yazid says that when Muadh ibn Jabal used to offer the tahajjud (pre-dawn) prayers, he used to say: 'O Allah! Eyes are asleep; stars are about to disappear while You are The Ever-Living and Sustainer! O Allah! My search for Paradise is slow and my flight from Hell is weak. O Allah! Give me a guidance from Your Presence that You will return to me on the Day of Judgement. You will not break Your promise.'[40]

Qasim ibn Bazzah says that someone who heard Ibn Omar recite Surah Mutaffifeen informed him that when Ibn Omar reached (verse 6): **'...the day when people will stand up to face The Lord of all the worlds,'** he wailed so much that he could not recite any further.[41]

Samir Ar-Rayahi says that his father informed him that Ibn Omar drank some cold water and wept intensely. 'Why are you crying so much?' He was asked. He replied: 'I have remembered a verse of the Quran:

---

[38] Ibid

[39] Ibid: 1/483 and Hilya: 1/118

[40] Ibid: 1/492

[41] Ibid

وَحِيلَ بَيْنَهُمْ وَبَيْنَ مَا يَشْتَهُونَ كَمَا فُعِلَ بِأَشْيَاعِهِم مِّن قَبْلُ ۚ إِنَّهُمْ كَانُوا۟ فِى شَكٍّ مُّرِيبٍۭ ﴿٥٤﴾

'And a barrier is made between them and their desires (Surah Saba: *54).'* And I realised that the people of Hell will only desire water:

وَنَادَىٰٓ أَصْحَـٰبُ ٱلنَّارِ أَصْحَـٰبَ ٱلْجَنَّةِ أَنْ أَفِيضُوا۟ عَلَيْنَا مِنَ ٱلْمَآءِ أَوْ مِمَّا رَزَقَكُمُ ٱللَّهُ ۚ قَالُوٓا۟ إِنَّ ٱللَّهَ حَرَّمَهُمَا عَلَى ٱلْكَـٰفِرِينَ ﴿٥٠﴾

'Pour on us some water or from that which Allah has given you.' (Surah A'araaf: 50)

Nafi' ﷺ says whenever Ibn Omar ﷺ recited the verse:

۞ أَلَمْ يَأْنِ لِلَّذِينَ ءَامَنُوٓا۟ أَن تَخْشَعَ قُلُوبُهُمْ لِذِكْرِ ٱللَّهِ وَمَا نَزَلَ مِنَ ٱلْحَقِّ وَلَا يَكُونُوا۟ كَٱلَّذِينَ أُوتُوا۟ ٱلْكِتَـٰبَ مِن

قَبۡلُ فَطَالَ عَلَيۡهِمُ ٱلۡأَمَدُ فَقَسَتۡ قُلُوبُهُمۡۖ وَكَثِيرٞ مِّنۡهُمۡ فَٰسِقُونَ ١٦

'Is it not time for the believers for their hearts to soften out of the remembrance of Allah,' (Surah Hadeed: 16) he used to cry so much that his weeping would overwhelm him.'[42]

Abdur-Rahnian ibn Abi Layla ﷺ narrates from Abu Dharr ﷺ: 'By Allah! If you knew what I knew you would not find joy with your wives and you would not be able to relax on your beds. By Allah! I wish that Allah would have created me as a tree whose fruit is eaten.'[43]

Asad ibn Wada'ah ﷺ says that Shaddad ibn Auws ﷺ used to toss and turn in his bed without sleeping. He would say: 'O Allah! The fire has prevented me from sleeping,' and then resort to prayers until Fajr.[44] Asad ﷺ also mentioned that Shaddad ﷺ used to be like seeds in a frying pan…

Mujahid ﷺ says 'Ibn Zubair ﷺ used to be like a stick (in apprehension) while he was in salat.'[45]

Bakr ibn Muzm ﷺ says that Abu Musa Ash'ari ﷺ gave a sermon in Basra and mentioned Hell. He cried so much

---

[42] Ibid

[43] Ibid: *1/595*

[44] Ibid: 1/709

[45] Ibid: 1/765

that his tears fell on the pulpit. The audience also wept considerably that day[46]

Imraan ibn Husam ﷺ used to say: 'If only I were ashes that the wind would scatter.'[47]

Ali ﷺ describes the characteristics of the Companions: 'By Allah I have seen the Companions of the Prophet ﷺ such that I have not seen anybody like them today. They used to wake up as if they had ridden goats all night with their clothes and hair disheveled. They spent the night performing *ruku' and sajdah* for Allah, reciting the Book and alternating between their feet and foreheads. And when they awoke in the morn, they remembered Allah and remained like a tree (whose branches) swaying in the wind with their eyes pouring tears so much that they wet their clothes. Now, it seems as if people are going to sleep completely oblivious and unaware.'[48]

Hasan Al-Basari ﷺ describes the Companions as: 'Tolerant to the point that if the ignorant came upon them, they would not be imprudent. This was during the day. At night, they poured their tears across their cheeks and made their feet stand in the row of salat, hoping for their necks (selves) to be delivered.'[49]

Iman Ahmed ﷺ reports from Abu Hayyan Taymi ﷺ that he had heard for thirty years or more that Ibn Masood ﷺ

---

[46] Takhweef: 32

[47] Minahjus Salikeen: 326

[48] Ihya: 4/180

[49] Musannaf: 13/506

used to pass by those who blow into bellows (the blacksmiths) and would faint.

Sa'd ibn Al-Ahzam ﷺ says that he was with Ibn Masood ﷺ when he passed by the iron smiths who were taking out iron from the furnace. Ibn Masood ﷺ stared at them and cried.[50]

Hasan Al-Basari ﷺ describes the Companions: 'I have witnessed and accompanied a group of people who were never flattered by anything of this world which came to them, nor were they sorry about anything that passed them. In fact, the world was worth much less to them than the dirt which you tread. They would not have any clothes sewn for them throughout their lives, nor would they ask their wives to cook a meal for them. They would also not have anything between themselves and the earth (at night). I found them to act upon the Book of their Lord and the way of their Prophet. When night came upon them, then they would stand on the side of their bed mats and weep. Then, they would ask their Lord to deliver them..'

'If they performed a good deed, they would be happy, offer gratitude for it and ask Allah to accept it from them. If they made a mistake, it would grieve them and they would ask Allah to pardon them. By Allah, they remained this way..'[51]

Muadh ibn Ann ﷺ says that he was close to Juban when Riyah Al-Qaisi ﷺ passed by him after Maghrib. When the roads were clear he heard (Riyah) burst into tears and say: 'How long are you going to keep on coming for me O day

---

[50] Takhweef

[51] Ihya: 4/396 and Musannaf in brief: 13/506

and night? I don't know what is meant from me. We are for Allah, we are for Allah.' He kept on saying that until he disappeared from him.

Furat ibn Sulaiman ﵁ says that Hasan ﵁ used to say: 'The believers are a nation whose senses have become so humble that the ignorant find them to be sick. They are, by Allah, people of the inner senses. Don't you see that Allah says:

وَقَالُوا۟ ٱلْحَمْدُ لِلَّهِ ٱلَّذِىٓ أَذْهَبَ عَنَّا ٱلْحَزَنَ ۖ إِنَّ رَبَّنَا لَغَفُورٌ شَكُورٌ ﴿٣٤﴾

'They will say: 'All praise is due to Allah who has relieved us of our grief.' (Surah Fatir: 34)

By Allah, they have absorbed a great deal of grief in the world. But their grief is not what grieves people. However, they have grieved because of the fear of Hell.'[52]

Omar ﵁ heard a person in Tahajjud recite the verse:

'Indeed the punishment of your Lord is inevitable: there will be none to avert it.' (in Surah Toor: 7/8)

---

[52] Takhweef: 20

Omar said: 'Allah has made a true promise,' and returned home and became ill for a month. People visited him but did not know what his sickness was.[53]

Someone said: 'Grief prevents food and fear stops sins.'[54]

Hasan ﷺ used to say: 'Do not let the statement: 'A man is with whom he loves' deceive you. For you will never be with the pious except with their deeds. The Jews and Christians claim they love their prophets, but they will not be with them.'[55]

Shaqiq ibn Ibrahim ﷺ says: 'There is no better companion for a person than grief and fear: grief over the sins which passed and fear for the future what it might bring.

Amir ibn Qais ﷺ says: 'The people who will be the happiest in the Hereafter will be the ones who are the most concerned in this world (for the Hereafter). The people who will laugh the most will be the ones who have cried the most in this world (out of fear). The most sincere people as far as Iman is concerned will be the ones who are the most contemplative in this world.'[56]

---

[53] Ibid: 29

[54] Tanbeehul Ghafileen

[55] Ibid

[56] Ibid

Exhortation of the Predecessors to Taqwa[57]

My dear Muslim brother! You should be informed that the predecessors - may Allah be pleased with them - always exhorted one another towards taqwa.

Abu Bakr ﷺ used to say in his khutba: 'I advise you to observe taqwa and to praise Allah as He deserves to be praised. Mix hope with fear and combine importunity with asking (for help). Allah has praised Zakariyah ﷺ and his family: **'They used to race towards goodness, invoke Us with hope and fear and they were devout to Us.'**[58]

When Abu Bakr ﷺ was about to die, he called Omar ﷺ and advised him first and foremost to fear Allah.

Omar ﷺ wrote to his son: 'I advise you to fear Allah, for whoever fears Him has protected himself from His punishment. Whoever offers Him a loan, He will repay (reward) him and whoever thanks Him, He will give him more. Make taqwa your goal and the polish of your heart.

Ali ﷺ deputised someone for an expedition and said: 'I advise you to fear Allah Whom you have to meet and

---

[57] This Chapter is taken from Chapter 3 of *Taqwa: The Provision of Believers,* Al-Firdous Ltd, 1995.

[58] Surah Al-Anbiyaa: 90

besides Whom you have no destination. He controls the world and the Hereafter.'

Omar ibn Abdul Aziz wrote to a man: 'I advise you to observe fear of Allah Who accepts nothing except that (taqwa), Who shows mercy only to its adherents and Who rewards only on its account. There are many who preach it, but few who practice it. May Allah make us all among those who have taqwa.'

When Omar became khalifah he gave a sermon and said: 'I advise you to fear Allah and be good because He is with those who fear and do good.'

A man was about to leave for Hajj and asked Omar to advise him. He said: 'Fear Allah, for whoever fears Him will never feel lonely.'

Shu'ba says that whenever he used to prepare for a journey, he would ask Hakam if he (Hakam) required anything. He would say: 'I advise you with the words of the Prophet when he advised Muadh: 'Fear Allah wherever you are, follow up a mistake with kindness for it will erase it and approach people with good manners.'

A predecessor wrote to one of his brother: 'I advise you to fear Allah because it is the best thing you can hide, the most beautiful thing you can reveal and the most valuable thing you can treasure. May Allah help us both to observe it and give us both its reward.'

Another person wrote to his brother: 'I advise you and myself to observe taqwa for it is the best provision for the world and the Hereafter. Make it a means towards every good deed and a deterrent against every evil. Allah has guaranteed those with taqwa deliverance from their anxieties and provisions from unexpected quarters.[59]

When Ali ﷺ returned from the Battle of Siffin, he passed by a graveyard outside Kufa and said: 'O you who live in houses that create loneliness and in deserted places! You who live in darkening graves! O people of dust and alienation! O people of isolation and loneliness! You are, for us, scouts and we, for you, followers. The houses? Well, they have become inhabited again. The wives? They have remarried. The wealth? It has been distributed. This is the news we have for you. What news do you have for us? Then Ali ﷺ turned towards his army and said: 'If they were permitted to speak, they would inform you that the best provision is taqwa.'[60]

---

[59] The preceding quotations are from Jamiul Hikam: 194

[60] Nahjul Balagha: 126

TIME IS
RUNNING OUT
BEAST
CATASTROPHES BEFORE THE
DAY OF JUDGEMENT
IMAM SIDDIQ HASSAN KHAN

The Qualities of Those with Taqwa[61]

Allah has mentioned the qualities of those with taqwa (muttaqoon) many times throughout the Quran. He has described how they are pleasant, civil and they are of sound judgement. One of the most comprehensive verses in this regard is the verse of virtue (birr):

۞ لَّيْسَ ٱلْبِرَّ أَن تُوَلُّوا۟ وُجُوهَكُمْ قِبَلَ ٱلْمَشْرِقِ
وَٱلْمَغْرِبِ وَلَـٰكِنَّ ٱلْبِرَّ مَنْ ءَامَنَ بِٱللَّهِ وَٱلْيَوْمِ ٱلْـَٔاخِرِ
وَٱلْمَلَـٰٓئِكَةِ وَٱلْكِتَـٰبِ وَٱلنَّبِيِّـۧنَ وَءَاتَى ٱلْمَالَ عَلَىٰ
حُبِّهِۦ ذَوِى ٱلْقُرْبَىٰ وَٱلْيَتَـٰمَىٰ وَٱلْمَسَـٰكِينَ وَٱبْنَ
ٱلسَّبِيلِ وَٱلسَّآئِلِينَ وَفِى ٱلرِّقَابِ وَأَقَامَ ٱلصَّلَوٰةَ وَءَاتَى
ٱلزَّكَوٰةَ وَٱلْمُوفُونَ بِعَهْدِهِمْ إِذَا عَـٰهَدُوا۟ ۖ
وَٱلصَّـٰبِرِينَ فِى ٱلْبَأْسَآءِ وَٱلضَّرَّآءِ وَحِينَ ٱلْبَأْسِ ۗ أُو۟لَـٰٓئِكَ
ٱلَّذِينَ صَدَقُوا۟ ۖ وَأُو۟لَـٰٓئِكَ هُمُ ٱلْمُتَّقُونَ ﴿١٧٧﴾

[61] This Chapter is taken from Chapter 4 of *Taqwa: The Provision of Believers,* Al-Firdous Ltd, 1995.

'Virtue is not that you turn towards the East or the West. Virtue is (the virtue of) those who believe in Allah, the Last Day, the angels, the Revelation and the prophets; those who, for the love of Allah, give wealth to relatives, orphans, the needy, the wayfarer, those who ask and for those in captivity (like slaves); those who establish prayers and offer zakat; those who fulfill their promise after making one and those who are steadfast in trial, adversity and the time of war. They are the ones who are truthful and those are the ones who have taqwa'[62] ***(Al-Baqarah – 177)***

---

[62] SurahBaqarah: 177

Ali's Description of Those With Taqwa

Hamman ibn Shuraih - a companion of Ali ﵁ - asked him to narrate the qualities of the people of taqwa so that he would be able to see them in front of him. Ali ﵁ said: 'When Allah created His creation, He did so while He was completely independent of their obedience towards Him and of their disobedience towards Him. No disobedience can hurt Him and no obedience can benefit Him. Then He distributed amongst them (the creation) their means of sustenance and placed them on earth. The people of taqwa on earth are those of virtue: their speech is correct (true); their garments are of moderate nature and their walk is one of humility. They lower their gazes when they see something that Allah has forbidden them to see and they give an ear to beneficial knowledge. They maintain their ~integrity in both adversity and prosperity.

Had it not been for the appointed time that Allah has written for them (death), their souls would not remain an extra second in their bodies out of yearning for reward and fear of punishment. The Creator ranks Supreme in their eyes, so everything else becomes immaterial to them. They are with Paradise as if they had already witnessed it and enjoyed its presence. They are with Hell as if they have already seen it and tasted its torment. Their hearts grieve and their evil (if any) is non-contagious. Their bodies are lean, their needs are few and their souls are chaste.

They observe patience for a few days and experience ever-lasting comfort. This is a profitable exchange that their Lord has made pleasant for them. The world tempts them, but they do not succumb. It imprisons them, but they ransomed themselves in exchange.

During the nights they stand in rows and read portions of the Quran. They recite with proper recitation which I grieves their hearts and drink it (the Quran) like medicine. If a verse of yearning comes along, they reach for it and believe it is their destination. If an intimidating verse comes along, they pour their hearts towards it and believe that Hell and its screams are in their ears. They sleep on their foreheads and elbows[63] and implore Allah to deliver them.

In the day, they are tolerant and learned, kind and God-fearing. Fear has chipped away at their bodies as if they were arrows. Anyone looking at them would think that they were sick. But they are not sick. Some will say that they are confused. A great fear has made them look like that. They are never content to do only a few actions (during the day), nor do they ask for a great deal. They condemn themselves and are apprehensive about their deeds. If one of them is called "pious", he fears what will be said of him and says: 'I know myself better than you do. My Lord knows me better than I do. O Allah! Do not take me to task for what they are saying about me and (O Lord) make me better than they think. Forgive my sins which they do not know about.'

---

[63] i.e. they engage in prayers so much that it is as if they sleep in those postures

Their signs are that they are strong in Islam, resolute in their softness; firm in their belief. They crave for knowledge and are knowledgeable with tolerance; moderate in richness; pleasant in hunger; forbearing in distress; seeking halal; active in (pursuing) guidance and they abhor greed.

They perform good deeds in fear (of rejection). They spend the evening in gratitude and the morning in remembrance. They sleep in alarm and they awake in joy. If their carnal selves make it difficult for them to fulfill that which they dislike they deprive them (their selves) of that which they like. The apple of their eyes is in what does not perish and their abstemiousness is in what disappears. They combine knowledge with tolerance and speech with action.

You will find their hopes are realistic their mistakes few; their hearts humble their selves content; their diet meager their matters simple; their Deen safe-guarded, their desires killed and their anger subdued. Goodness is expected from them and evil is shielded against them. If they are among those who are oblivious, they are counted amongst those who remember (Allah). If they are among those who remember, they are not written among the oblivious. They pardon those who wrong them; they provide for those who deprive them and meet those who severe ties with them. They are never profane and always lenient. Their wrong doings are almost non-existent and their good deeds are always present. They are resolute when the earth quakes, steadfast in calamities and grateful in prosperity.

They are not prejudiced against those they dislike nor do they favour those they love. They acknowledge the truth before it appears and do not lose anything they are entrusted with. They do not call anyone names nor do they hurt their neighbours. They do not curse at the time of difficulties nor do they venture into falsehood.

Silence does not bother them and if they laugh they do not raise their voices. If they are treated with injustice they remain patient until Allah vindicates them.

Their own selves live in toil while others are comfortable around them.

Their abstinence from those who stay away from them is their exoneration (from malice). Their proximity to those who are close to them is a means of mercy (for those who are close to them). Their remaining aloof is not out of pride and arrogance and their being close is neither a ploy nor a scheme.[64]

---

[64] Nahjul Balagha: 241

The Final Moment
THE CALAMITY OF DEATH
By Dr. Aaid Ibn Abdullah al-Qarni

Wahid Abdussalam Bali

Do You Think
You Have Sihr, Jinn or Evil Eye?
NOW
AVAILABLE
Honey
Ruqya
with honey
Ruqya with
Olive Oil
Ruqya with water
and sidr leaves
Ruqya CD
Please contact:
Brother Abdul Majid
and he will help you by the Mercy of Allah
07983725705 / 07525473283

Sultan Muhammad
Al-Fatih

Dr Ali Muhammad Al-Salaabi

Wonderful
Scientific Signs
in the Qur'aan
DR. ZAGHLOUL AN-NAJJAR

33 Ways To
Concentrate
In Your
PRAYER
REFLECTING
REMEMBERING DEATH
TRANQUILLITY IN SALAH
MUHAMMAD SALIH AL-MUNAJJID

The Islamic Concept
Of
Justice
Written by: Umar Ahmed Kassir